MAR – – 2015

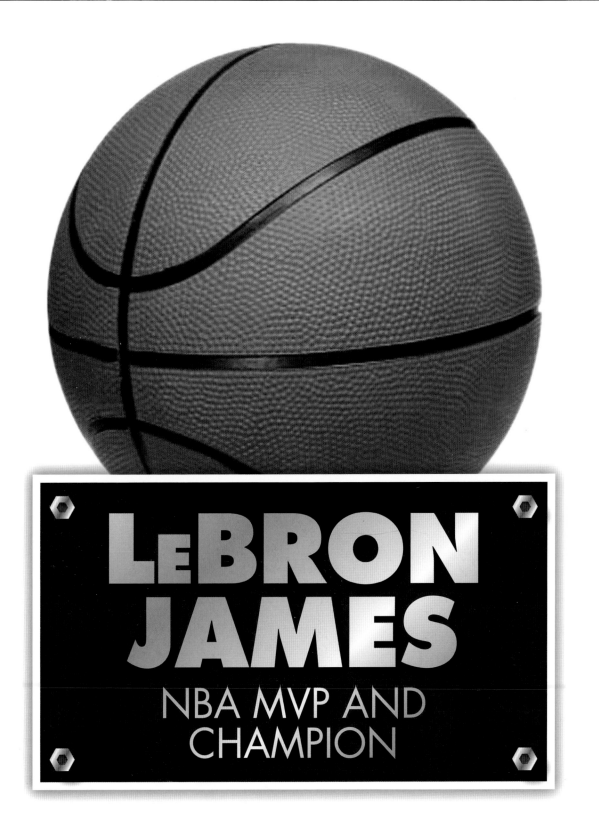

LeBRON JAMES

NBA MVP AND CHAMPION

BY MAXWELL HAMMER

The Child's World®

Published by The Child's World®
1980 Lookout Drive • Mankato, MN 56003-1705
800-599-READ • www.childsworld.com

ACKNOWLEDGMENTS
The Child's World®: Mary Berendes, Publishing Director
Red Line Editorial: Editorial direction
The Design Lab: Design
Amnet: Production
Design Elements: Reisio
Photographs ©: Manu Fernandez/AP Images, cover; Zuma
Press/Icon SMI, 5; J.D. Pooley/AP Images, 7; Bruce Schwartz-
man/AP Images, 9; Tony Dejak/AP Images, 11, 13; Kelvin
Ma/Icon SMI, 15; J Pat Carter/AP Images, 17; Lynne Sladky/
AP Images, 19, 21

ISBN 9781631437373
LCCN 2014945306

Printed in the United States of America
Mankato, MN
November, 2014
PA02239

ABOUT THE AUTHOR

Maxwell Hammer grew up in the Adirondacks of New York before becoming an international sports reporter and children's book author. When not traveling the world on assignment, he spends his winters in Thunder Bay, Ontario, with his wife and pet beagle.

TABLE OF CONTENTS

CHAPTER 1

STAR AMONG STARS

LeBron James stepped onto the court on a mission. It was the 2013 National Basketball Association (NBA) Finals. His Miami Heat were down three games to two. The San Antonio Spurs needed just one more win for the title. James wasn't about to let that happen.

At 6'8" and 250 pounds, James is an athletic wonder. He can outrun, out-jump, and overpower just about any opponent. James can also read and react to game action faster than others. His skill set is one of a kind. James can thrive as a point guard or power forward.

On this night, those amazing abilities showed. James scored 32 points, grabbed 10 **rebounds**, and passed out 11 **assists**. It was his second **triple-double** in the series. The Heat won 103–100. Two days later, James scored 37 points as Miami won the NBA title. He was also named NBA Finals Most Valuable Player (MVP).

James had an incredible stat line in the 2013 NBA Finals. He ended with averages of 43 minutes, 25.3 points, 10.9 rebounds, 7.0 assists, and 2.3 steals per game.

James dribbles through the San Antonio Spurs during Game 6 of the 2013 NBA Finals on June 18, 2013.

CHAPTER 2

YOUNG IN AKRON

Life was often hard for LeBron growing up in Akron, Ohio. His mom, Gloria, was only 16 when LeBron was born on December 30, 1984. Gloria didn't have much money. LeBron's dad wasn't around to help. So Gloria and LeBron moved around a lot when he was young.

Everything changed for LeBron when he was in fourth grade. LeBron moved in with another family, the Walkers. They offered him stability and taught him discipline. They also introduced him to basketball.

LeBron has never met his dad, Anthony McClelland. However, LeBron later thanked his dad. He said that McClelland's absence inspired him to succeed.

LeBron hugs his mother after a tournament win for his high school team on March 15, 2003.

CHAPTER 3

HIGH SCHOOL PHENOM

LeBron gained a loyal group of friends through basketball. The same group played together for seven years.

By eighth grade, NBA **scouts** had taken notice of LeBron's basketball skills. Fans packed the gyms to watch his monster dunks. When LeBron was a junior, *Sports Illustrated* put him on the cover. The headline called him "The Chosen One."

He and his friends went 102–6 and won three state titles in four years of high school.

LeBron was a high school all-state wide receiver in football. Many believe he could have played in the National Football League.

LeBron was a star for St. Vincent-St. Mary High School in Akron, Ohio.

CHAPTER 4

CALLED BY THE CAVS

James entered the NBA **Draft** straight out of high school. The hometown Cleveland Cavaliers (the Cavs) selected him first overall in the 2003 draft. The Cavs were one of the league's worst teams. Fans believed James could finally lead the team to a title.

They would have to be patient, though. James was just 18 years old. And the Cavs would need more than one star player to change their luck.

The Cavs averaged 18,288 fans at home games during James's **rookie** season. That was up from just 11,497 the year before.

The Cavaliers chose James with the first pick of the 2003 NBA Draft.

CHAPTER 5

NBA FINALISTS

James was a starter from Day 1. He made his first All-Star Game in his second year. In his third year, James led the Cavs to the playoffs. Expectations in Cleveland were sky-high. Then, in 2006–07, James led the team to the NBA Finals. It was the team's first NBA Finals in its 37-year history.

The series only showed James and the Cavs how far they had to go, though. James had been one of the league's top players that season. Nobody played more minutes. Only Kobe Bryant scored more points. Yet the Cavs hardly had a chance in the NBA Finals. The San Antonio Spurs swept them in four games.

James had another milestone in 2004 when he made the U.S. Olympic team. Team USA's bronze medal marked its worst Olympic finish since it started using professional players. But James made up for it with gold medals in 2008 and 2012.

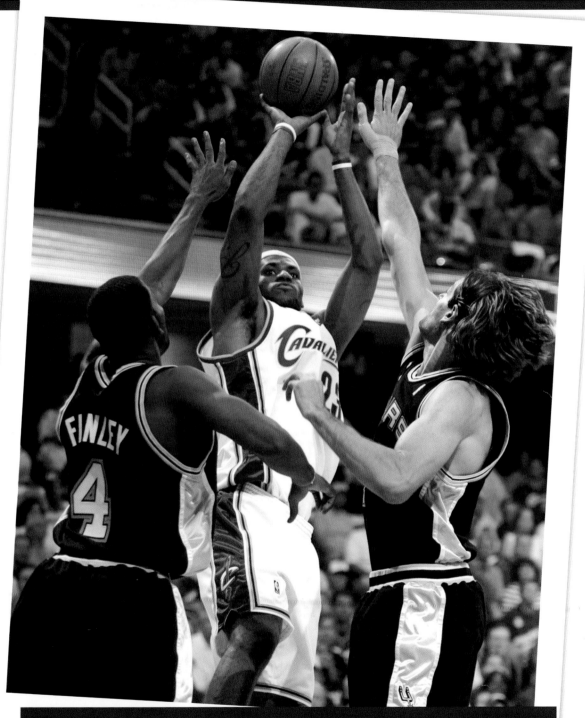

James (center) shoots over a pair of San Antonio Spurs players during Game 4 of the NBA Finals on June 14, 2007.

CHAPTER 6

LEADER OF THE CAVS

Cavaliers fans couldn't be too upset about the loss. James had not yet turned 23 by the start of the 2007-08 season. Surely he would lead them back to another NBA Finals. He certainly tried. James won his first scoring title that season. He won his first two NBA MVP Awards in 2008-09 and 2009-10. The kid from Akron, Ohio, was now a bona fide superstar.

But returning to the NBA Finals was a much more difficult task. The Cavs only reached the conference finals one more time through 2010. It was a frustrating time for James and the Cleveland fans.

James is known for his great offensive abilities. He also became a standout defender. Through 2013–14 James was named to the NBA All-Defensive First Team six times.

James reacts to a call by referees in a game against the Boston Celtics on April 4, 2010.

CHAPTER 7

THE DECISION

James was a **free agent** after the 2009-10 season. Every team in the NBA wanted to sign him. Fans and media members tried to guess where James would sign. That summer, he decided to make his announcement on live TV. The special program was called *The Decision*. In announcing his choice, James famously said, "I'm going to take my talents to South Beach and join the Miami Heat."

Some good came out of *The Decision*. The event raised more than $2 million for various charities.

It was supposed to be a moment of celebration. And for Miami Heat fans it was. But many people were angry with James. They felt that he turned his back on Cleveland. Worse, though, was that he did so on national TV.

James (6) joined fellow superstars Dwyane Wade (3) and Chris Bosh (1) to play for the Miami Heat.

CHAPTER 8

HOT AND COLD

James made a prediction before the 2010-11 season. He said the Heat would win multiple NBA titles. They got off to a slow start, though. Miami started the season 9-8. Finally the Heat's three stars—Chris Bosh, James, and Dwyane Wade—came together. They cruised all the way to the NBA Finals. The Heat players were confident they'd win. They didn't, though. The Dallas Mavericks beat the Heat in six games.

James did some soul-searching that offseason. He had not expected the negative backlash from *The Decision*. The entire year had left him humbled. So James set out to improve his attitude. He also set out to improve his game. He called Hall of Fame center Hakeem Olajuwon for help.

Chris Bosh also signed with the Heat in 2010. James and Bosh joined Heat star Dwyane Wade. They had become friends while playing for Team USA over the years.

James leaps for a dunk against the Indiana Pacers on February 8, 2011.

CHAPTER 9

BACK-TO-BACK CHAMPS

James came into the 2011–12 season as a changed man and a changed player. Outside distractions no longer got in the way of his basketball career. And working with Olajuwon made a huge difference. James was able to use his big, athletic body under the basket like never before.

James easily won his third MVP Award. The NBA Finals was a battle between the league's two biggest stars, James and Oklahoma City Thunder forward Kevin Durant. The series left little question who was the king. James led the Heat to a five-game victory. Then he hit the trifecta again the next year: NBA MVP, NBA Finals champion, and NBA Finals MVP.

A bid for a three-peat was thwarted in 2014. James was second in MVP voting. The San Antonio Spurs beat the Heat in an NBA Finals rematch.

On July 11, 2014, James announced that he was returning to Cleveland to play for the Cavaliers again. Cavaliers fans were ecstatic to welcome James back. The low-key announcement in *Sports Illustrated* was much humbler than *The Decision* of 2010. "I'm ready to accept the challenge. I'm coming home," James said.

James (left) holds the NBA Finals MVP trophy while teammate Dwyane Wade holds the Championship Trophy after the Heat's victory over the Spurs in Game 7 of the 2013 NBA Finals.

FUN FACTS

LᴇBRON JAMES

BORN: December 30, 1984

HOMETOWN: Akron, Ohio

TEAMS: Cleveland Cavaliers (2003–10, 2014–), Miami Heat (2010–2014)

POSITIONS: Small forward, power forward, shooting guard

HEIGHT: 6′8″

WEIGHT: 240 pounds

NBA FINALS (WINS IN BOLD): 2007, 2011, **2012, 2013,** 2014

OLYMPIC GAMES (GOLD MEDALS IN BOLD): 2004, **2008, 2012**

ALL-STAR APPEARANCES: 10 (2005–14)

AWARDS

   NBA MVP: 2008–09, 2009–10, 2011–12, 2012–13

   NBA FINALS MVP: 2012, 2013

   ROOKIE OF THE YEAR: 2003–04

GLOSSARY

assists (uh-SISTS) Assists are passes that lead directly to a basket. James had a career-high 651 assists in 2009–10.

draft (draft) Professional teams scout and select new players to join their rosters in the draft. The Cavaliers chose James first overall in the 2003 NBA Draft.

free agent (free AY-juhnt) A player who is not signed to a team is a free agent. James was a free agent after the 2009–10 and 2013–14 seasons.

rebounds (REE-boundz) Rebounds are recoveries of missed shots. James had 533 rebounds in the 2013–14 season.

rookie (RUK-ee) A player in his or her first year in a new league is a rookie. LeBron James was a star rookie for the Cavaliers.

scouts (skouts) People who watch basketball games and evaluate talent are scouts. Scouts took note of James's talent in high school.

triple-double (TRIP-uhl DUHB-uhl) A triple-double is when a player records double digits (at least 10) in at least three of five stat categories: points, rebounds, assists, steals, and blocked shots. James's first triple-double was on January 19, 2005.

TO LEARN MORE

BOOKS

Doeden, Matt. *NBA Dynasties*. Mankato, MN: Accelerate, 2013.

Hill, Anne E. *LeBron James: King of Shots*. Minneapolis, MN: Twenty-First Century Books, 2013.

Morreale, Marie. *LeBron James*. New York: Children's Press, an Imprint of Scholastic Inc., 2014.

Smallwood, John. *Megastars 2011*. New York: Scholastic, 2011.

WEB SITES

Visit our Web site for links about LeBron James:

childsworld.com/links

Note to Parents, Teachers, and Librarians: We routinely verify our Web links to make sure they are safe and active sites. So encourage your readers to check them out!

INDEX